Love Life: Poems Inspired by The Rutles

Jen Selinsky

*Not every poem included in this book is dated in chronological order. This is not an oversight on my part. Rather, I have made some changes and substitutions.

-J.L.S.

Not to be taken

Seriously for

Every move which

You can make

With instruments;

The lyrics which

Are placed on

Top of its mad

Howling and

Barking, carrying

On like there

Is no tomorrow.

4/1/14

It is to be

Placed in your

Vault of treasures,

Saving it for

Those whom you

Want to know;

Closer in hopes

Of letting *one*

Know that they

Mean the world

To you!

4/1/14

Obvious message;

I want to make

This as painless

As possible.

There's no way

That we are

Meant to be

Together, yet

You want to

Rub it all in

My face.

Clean break now!

4/2/14

What part

Of you is ashamed

To be with me?

Not even a

Finger to move

In my direction,

Let alone a

Hand.

Why can't we

Make this

How it's all

Meant to be,

Instead of you

Holding out

On me?

4/2/14

No way to leave

This out, even

Though I am not

One to credit

Some early

Influences.

Not a piece of

Information that

I want to

Divulge but,

If I don't,

People everywhere

Are going to

Shake their

Heads in confusion.

4/2/14

Feeling through

And counting on

Actions; this is

More than I can

Display in some

Kind of video,

Though you will

Have to see

For yourself.

4/2/14

Reaching out

To the lesser

Branches; you

Couldn't believe

That I knew

All the words

To poems I

Never knew

Existed before,

All part of

My expanding

Knowledge!

4/2/14

Too far away,

More than I

Would like to

Remember the

Date, but all

Is well, and I

Can see the

Same familiarity

As with a

Comfortable, old

Pair of shoes,

Which has

Not even come

Close to wearing

Out, nor will

They ever!

4/2/14

Back to home;

I do not want

To speak so

Bluntly about

A man who

Has done so

Much for us.

And the

Depression

Shall never

Spread because

He is stronger

Than anything

Which can be

Thrown in his

Direction; God

Created him

To be so!

4/2/14

One of

The parts

I liked best

About you;

Quick was I

To gain

Fascination,

Especially

Because you

Are both

New and

Old at the

Same time.

Great to

Rediscover

All the

Paths which

We have been

Explored

Before.

4/2/14

So slow

Compared

To what

I used to

Hear before,

But I did

Not have

All the

Right reasons

To be

Disappointed,

Especially

Because your

Art was

Constant

And present.

4/2/14

Not the

Same street

Which you

Are accustomed

To hearing

About in all

The songs

You know

And love.

Still, people

Gathered and

Wanted to

Know all

Your history.

4/2/14

Never stopping

Before I reach

My destination

Because all I

Can see will

Not be achieved

By me sitting

Tight on my

Laurels!

4/2/14

Can't believe

That I was

Able to move

On to the

Next level

While all

The world

Was watching

And making

Me realize

Wait! You

Are not

Who I

Originally

Thought

You to

Be!

4/2/14

Now, you

Come back

After teasing

Me, thinking

Back to when

You were

Present in

My life before.

4/2/14

Going back

To an old

Classic; this

Can only be

As good as

I remembered

It all

To be.

No way to

Think about

How you

Could have

Hidden

Yourself

From me,

Even

A small

Bout

Of inactivity.

All which

You claimed

To be has

Redefined,

How

I looked at

You after

I grew older.

4/2/14

Such a way

To make

Flattery; how

I could

Identify only

After having

Known a

Little

Portion,

The smallest

Not being

Greater or

Less than

Because of

Someone

Who

Can find

Delightful

Humor in

Something so

Parodied is

Always eager

To show how

It has

Caught

On to the

Humor.

4/2/14

Large words

And how they

Care defines.

I did not know

Until I had

The ability to

Look things up.

Extrapolating

Meaning from

One thing is

Actually

Easier than

It seems!

4/2/14

Ah! There

You are;

I'm waiting

In the folds

Of the crowd,

Who had to

Stay in the

Back because

They dare

Not be seen.

But you know

That you will

Want to call

On me when

The time is

Most right.

4/2/14

Still room

For

Comparison;

They

Are not

Quite as

Similar as

They seem,

Especially

When

You take

The time

To read

Into all

The meaning

And are not

Forced by

Anything

But plain

Curiosity,

Driven as

What we

Are, human

Beings.

4/2/14

Can you

Say that

You're

Impressed

That I've

Made it

This far?

No records

Have been

Forged

Today,

But all has

Been

To make

Me feel like

I've done

Something

More

Valuable

With my

Time than

Sit and

Stare at

The space.

4/2/14

Such an age

When I thought

Of myself as

Most Bohemian;

More than half

My years have

Built up since

Then, but I

Still think

Of myself in

That body,

Circling the

Globe with

My arms

Outstretched to

Embrace life

And let

Everyone know

About my

Presence!

4/2/14

Not quite the

Same feel, but

How can I refuse

Something which

I have sought

(All those years

Ago)?

Definition of

New meaning

Before I had

To move and,

Now, I am

Happy to

Include you

Where I was

So hesitant

Before.

4/2/14

Too silly,

What would

Others say if

They knew

That my

Fingers cramp

Up at such

"Nonsense" as

Some would

Say, but who

And I to

Question comedy

In its finest

Moment?

4/2/14

Some people

Dismissed you as

A novelty, but

You are far much

More than that.

Beloved is a parody

That can touch the

Hearts of many

With words designated

To a certain audience.

How can the cynical

Hearts not recognize

The talent which is

So abundant, the

Talent which took you

Years to build up

With every breath

Of your soul,

Whether you took

It seriously or not.

I have gone no

Further out of my way

To try and explain,

For this is a case

Where I have to

Let my words

Speak for themselves.

Showcasing a lesser

Known talent is not

Always easy,

But I feel that it

Must be done,

Nonetheless.

5/7/17

Electric sounds

Bring me back to

The day when I thought

I would never make

A name for myself,

But my light did

Not burn any less

Bright.

It has always been

That way, and I

Can find a time to

Reminisce to the tune

Of something which

Can always make

Me smile.

It has given me

Time to think of how

Far both of us have

Come during a time

When folks like us

Still have a difficult

Time reaching those

Whom we deem

Worthy of experiencing

Our material in a

Different light.

It has come to stand,

The day when people

Must walk the fine

Line between that which

Is serious and that

Which gives our hearts

Reason to smile.

5/7/17

You can say

That I am

Quite the opposite,

Afraid of many

Interactions

Which aren't

Required.

If you can

Understand

Even a small

Fraction of

What I live,

Then you

Would come to,

Or go, far away

From me.

4/2/14

So much of

My life's works

Unfinished; there

Had to be a

Remedy to that,

And I know

What everyone

Tries to say

When I wear

Myself down

To the nub.

Always some

Kind of break

Mentioned in

The fever

Which has

Already turned

My skin

Pale.

4/2/14

Help me find

The words to say

When there is a

Lack of something

Moving, pushing

Further against

All hope.

I know what

They mean

When they say

How music

Can fill the

Void for a

Quick pick-

Me-up.

4/2/14

No way

That I want

To leave all

This alone,

Even though

I tried to show

Myself the

Door, always

Finding my

Way back

Inside.

4/2/14

Asking for a

Stop far too soon.

It gets me going

Enough I have

Entitled myself a

Chance to sit

Back and enjoy

Thru the frothy

Thrill of victory.

4/2/14

When again,

Another moment,

I shall compare

You to another

Barking dog.

Nothing much to

Do with how

It keeps me

Thinking bizarre

Thoughts, something

Very similar

To what your

Mind had

Hatched all

Those years ago.

4/2/14

Can you blame

A person

For trying?

Is there

Any way

I can get you to

Reply to my

Tongue-tied

Response?

When I said

All that was

In my heart,

You did

Nothing but

Blink and

Put your finger to

Your chin,

Like you were

Trying to think;

Sudden cause

For dismissal.

I'd say that

You were saved

By the bell.

4/2/14

Once thought

You did not mean

To sound like your

Counterpart,

Musing on that

Until I heard

The true words

Echoing about

Being stuck in

The middle

Statistics to

Reach my

Physical presence,

Though they

Can never

Have my brain,

Which thinks

Outside the

Gray matter!

4/2/14

Not for everyone

To pass around,

Though the public

Can share.

I don't really

Fetch the

Concept, though

The sound gives

Me a hippy

Mentality and

Makes me

Wonder what

It would have been

Like to live in

A commune

Sometime

Shortly after

The second

Half of the

Twentieth century.

4/2/14

One of my

Favorites

Mixed

In with your

Crowd.

Not much

Longer until

I discovered

His

Genius,

And I want

To live,

Knowing

That

You have

Fed each

Other.

No point in

Saying that

Originality

Is overrated,

But the best

Ideas tend

To come

From each

Other's best

Features.

4/2/14

Trying to announce

Another part of my

Fresh being; you

Struck a chord

Which brought me

Back to the days of yore!

All I have to do is

Keep my eyes open,

Or closed, and my

Mind wide enough

To receive visions

From the past.

4/2/14

Forgetting the

Sound, though it

Shall come back

To me very soon,

Blasting into my

Head like whatever

Exists tomorrow

Can only pale

Compared to the

Rich flavors of

What was sampled

Today.

4/2/14

Adjustments

For something

That keeps

Spinning and

Changing all

The time.

Planet not

As lonely as

It would like

Most to think,

And digital

Mind-

Frame has

Come into

My life,

Although

A little late.

But I shall

Not be quiet

About the

Date because

I find that

Having no

Voice makes

One weak

And

Mistrusting.

4/2/14

Almost too close

To label you as

Something different,

And this is the

Perfect time to

Reminisce.

Young ones eager

To listen, but

Not long enough

To send a

 Barrage of questions

Coming your way.

Then, their little

Minds try to

Comprehend the

Time right before

They make up

One of their own.

4/2/14

Parlez-vous Français?

Now, I can barely

Speak the Queen's

English while living

Here in the U.S.A.

Not sure of the

Words; I shall have

To look them up

And see what you

Are trying to

Mean, whether

In earnest or

In jest.

4/2/14

Not such

A thing

That I want

To describe.

Let someone

Else do it

Justice,

(For once).

4/2/14

Dermal relations

And how our

Vital outer organ

Is formed.

Red on the flesh

Will not last as

Long as someone

Would fear.

Keep nothing

Under wraps

For too long,

Lest you

Do not get

A chance to

Breathe and

Heal properly.

4/2/14

Getting most

Lazy, I shan't

Bother to even

Put a modern

Twist on this

Work formed

Not too long

Before I was

Born.

It has nothing

To do with

Vivid description,

Though I love

How everything

Is presented in

Such a neat

Package, at

Least until

Opened!

4/2/14

I have to think

About the future

In terms of all the

Great things I have

Yet to accomplish,

Instead of labelling

Burdens inside my

Mind.

Worlds awakened

Will have new

appreciation for

What they can

Achieve through

Many means of

Inspiration.

5/7/17

I have to ask; I have

To gather a certain

Amount of information

Because there is

Nothing that I already

Know.

People don't like to

Be stopped, unless

It's something important.

Still, people have

Wages to earn, and

The means are not

Getting any more

Tasteful.

5/7/17

I have arrived in the

Country of my

Dreams (my home

Away from home).

All those years

Of dreaming were

Not lived in vain,

As I am proof that

Patience really

Does pay off.

I wonder what those

From this land of

Such great history

Will think of me,

Being from the colonies,

Ancestors cast off

In a different

Direction all those

Centuries ago.

But I have no direct

Proof that those from

Whom I descended

Were babies who came

Abroad on the famous

Ship, as a result of

All the April rain.

Will they disregard

Me as some kind of

Some lazy Yank

Who had no say

About the finer

Things in life, or

Will their fascination

Draw them closer

Into the deep recesses

Of my mind?

Only time shall

Tell, and time is

What I have most

Of now that I have

Arrived at my

Newest destination.

5/7/17

Bring me back to

Your music, the

Basic notes before

They were filled in

With words.

I know that the purity

Of it all has something

To do with the fact

That you found such

Sounds which are

Both delicate and

Intense.

And whether or not

They matched the parts

Which you designated

Later does not matter

In the slightest; you've

Got to hold onto your

Solid sounds!

People must know

Your roots so that

They have something

To gather when they

Discover all which

You mean for them

To hide in messages

Which one has to be

Most careful when

Deciphering for

Young and eager minds.

5/7/17

I should not to be

Too anxious to skip ahead,

Even though the possibilities

Are endless.

I have to take my time;

I have to sit with my

Hands on my lap

And wait for certain

Moments to pass by

Before the sun will

Shine in my corner.

I'd like to keep away

The rain, but it is

Just as essential to

Life, as the warm ball

In the sky with its

Healing rays.

Yet I know that

It's coming; I know

That it's always going

To find a way inside

My life and give me

What I need.

Favors, both asked

And unasked, will

Be my favor through

The grace of God.

5/7/17

I can only move forward and

Know that love truly does

Exist.

Evolution cannot explain

Emotions; nothing could ever

Replace what Jesus has

Done for us!

There is the brightness

Of days that have yet

To grace my presence.

And loneliness shall

Not plague me because

The Spirit is always here

And explains what I need

To feel in the absence

Of what is considered

A good day.

There is nothing that

These notes can take

Away, even as I am

Listening to them

During the time which

Is moving forward and

Making it so that

There is nothing to

Hide for fear or shame.

Natural therapy which

Can only make me

Gain.

5/7/17

Another part of you

Which reminds me of

Something from the

Recent past, so recent

That it was completed

Not very long ago.

I have no doubt that

The other has heard

Of you.

If not, then you

Might find it rewarding

To discover someone

Who has a means of

Spreading notes the

Same way as you.

It shall not take too

Long, as people find

Out about each other

By similar means

All the time.

Try it so that you

Might make another

Connection and

Brighten someone's

Day so that they will

Not have to hold down

Their head in shame.

Nothing would be

The same, and that is

A good thing.

5/7/17

I forgot all about

The greatness of

Your presence,

Until I had been

Called to come

Revisit it as

Something new.

Oh, I remember.

Yes, I remember

The great parts

Of you which

I have heard

Before, but there

Is something which

One can perceive

Through seasoned

Listening that he or she

Might not have picked

Up before.

It has been said

Before, but I now

Know the truth of

Such things now

That I am getting

Older.

It does not take long

For many to follow

What I say, even

Though time has a

Reason to shift

Much to the favor

Of youth these days.

But I am glad that

I had the opportunity

To see things for

A second, third, or

Even fourth time.

There is still a sense

 Of great mystery.

5/7/17

Now we must have to

Say goodbye, even

Though I don't want

To part company

With your wisdom.

5/7/17

Yet you will come

Back to me, and we'll

Make each other

Aware of all which

We have shared

Throughout the years…

5/7/17

About the Author

Jen Selinsky was born in Pittsburgh, PA. In 2003, she earned her bachelor's degree in English from Clarion University of Pennsylvania. In 2004, she earned her master's degree in library science from the same school. Jen has worked as a professional librarian for over eleven years. She has published more than 170 books, many of which contain poetry. Her work can be found on the following sites: Lulu, Amazon, Barnes & Noble, Kobo, iTunes, Smashwords, Pen It! Publications, and Buy Me Books Now. She has also been featured in publications such as: *The Courier Journal*, *Explorer* Magazine, *Liphar* Magazine, and *Indiana Libraries*. Jen lives in Sellersburg, IN with her husband.